The stature of Mau Mau leader Dedan Kimathi at the intersession of Kimathi and Mama Ngina Street in Nairobi's CBD.

Contents

Contributors
Muchemi Wachira
Gatu Mbaria

Cartoonist
Samuel Muigai

Photography
Billy Mutai
Simon Waruingi

Design & Layout
Barnabas Kimani

The Chronicles is a publication of Chronicles Communications,
P.O. Box 40942 - 00100,
Nairobi, Kenya
Pioneer House, Kenyatta Avenue,
2nd Floor,
Email: info@thechronicles.co.ke
Website. www.thechronicles.co.ke

A past too painful to share?

In the aftermath of the August 1st, 1982 attempted coup in Kenya, Maina Wa Kinyatti, by then a history lecturer at Kenyatta University was arrested in a crackdown on perceived government dissidents.

He was in the list of scholars and researchers wanted by the State for his role in authoring an academic thesis whose content did not go well with the Kanu administration under the late President, Daniel Arap Moi.

The government ostensibly felt offended by the history that portrayed country's rulers as turncoats and betrayers of the struggle to free Kenya from the hands of the British Colonial regime.

Kinyatti had researched and documented the history of the Mau Mau Revolution than any other scholar had done. This, as it is today, is a very sensitive subject in Kenya that often triggers public debate with people asking whether it was right for the government to treat the war veterans the way it did.

The Mau Mau Movement had been banned and branded dangerous. Anyone revisiting the history of the movement would rub the authoritarian government the wrong way.

This is how the good scholar fell victim to the dreaded security intelligence known at the time known as the Special Branch.

They raided his home looking for his written works and when they found a single page fact sheet amongst some of his personal documents, titled "Moi divisive tactics exposed", they arrested him - and charged him in court for being in possession of seditious document.

The court found the University lecturer guilty and sentenced him to six and half years' imprisonment.

Before him, other scholars and writers had found themselves in a similar fate. These were the dark days when government critics were subjected to all kinds of ill-treatment.

To avoid the cruelty meted out by the then Kanu regime, not many freedom fighters felt free to share some of their good and painful experiences during the struggle for independence.

There're also several senior citizens, who besides working for the Colonial Government, were sympathizers of the Mau Mau. They've untold stories. Some of these narratives may shape the history of Kenya.

But who'll help to recount them? This is what the Chronicles is attempting to do - telling some of the stories and personal accounts from people who participated in liberating Kenya from the Colonial rule. T

There's for example very little known about freedom fighters like, Koitalel Arap Samoei – the Orkoiyot or the supreme chief of the Nandi who resisted the British occupation. Same with Mekatilili Wa Menza – the women leader from the Girima community who also led a rebellion against the foreigners.

Although our historians and writers have written about Dedan Kimathi, who led the Mau Mau Revolution, very little is known about his international networks, which had won him admiration world over.

During his first visit to Kenya, former South African President Nelson Mandela confirmed Kimathi's global fame - to the surprise of many. He had managed to create his own global networks through letters he used to write for various publications in countries like India, United Kingdom and the US.

Not many know this. For instance, it is not in the knowledge of many Kenyans that Jawaharial Nehru – one of Kimathi's associates had to use his influence when he served as the Prime Minister of India to help the children of his colleague freedom fighter access education.

Most of the freedom heroes and heroines are long gone and the few who are alive – are in their twilight years. We are encouraging them to share their past experiences with the Chronicles. Such experiences can only be worthwhile if they're written and communicated – and shared with the subsequent generations.

Help me bury my husband before I die, Kimathi's widow cries out

Mukami Kimathi to Uhuru Kenyatta: help me bury my husband before I die

By The Chronicles Reporter

Dedan Kimathi's widow – Eloise Mukami - has renewed her appeal to the Kenyan Government to help her in exhuming the remains of her husband so she could give him a decent burial.

An ailing Mrs Kimathi, who now feels old age is catching up with her, wants the process of honouring the Independence war hero to be taken seriously. Efforts to identify Kimathi's grave have in the past proved futile.

The only available information from the Kenyan government is that the freedom fighter was buried in an unmarked grave – at Kamiti Maximum Prison – after he was hanged.

A Colonial court had found him guilty of being in possession of an illegal firearm before sentencing him to death. Mrs Kimathi believes that the British Government knows where her husband's grave is.

"I know the records are there showing where the grave is. I appeal to President Uhuru Kenyatta, his deputy (William Ruto) and Raila Odinga to ask the British Government to identify the grave so that I can bury his remains before I die," she pleaded while addressing a gathering of ex-freedom fighters at a function in Nairobi recently.

The function was organised by the Dedan Kimathi Foundation where she is the patron. Mrs Kimathi, who is now permanently confined in a wheelchair, said she was hopeful that the Kenyan Government would take her appeal seriously.

She reminded Kenyans that her husband, who was hanged when she was in detention for being a member of the Mau Mau, did not go to the forest for personal gain. "He went to the forest to

Kimathi's widow, Eloise Mukami speaks during Dedan Kimathi 62nd-Commemoration Gala Night at Uhuru Gardens, Nairobi recently.

free our country from slavery because he loved people and feared God," she said.

She also dispelled the notion some scholars have been advancing that Kimathi and the Mau Mau movement he led was only focused on getting back land that had been taken from members the Gikuyu community, by the white settlers.

"Kimathi was not fighting for Kikuyus but for Kenya and the entire East African region," said the freedom fighter who is now in her late 80's, as she noted that like Kimathi, most of those who sacrificed their lives for the country's independence have never been honoured and thus have never enjoyed the fruits of independence.

"Look at other countries – freedom fighters got rewards. And what happened to Kenya's freedom fighters? Most of them did not secure jobs. Some still have bullets lodged in their bodies and they live in misery."

She went on: "Let our government remember the Mau Mau, who spent their time in the forest – exposed to harsh weather conditions. I am sure this time our government is willing to assist." Mrs Kimathi further told her colleagues – most, like her, in their 80's, that Kenya has enough resources for all its citizens.

"If Kenya is not rich, the British would not have colonised us – and even today they are still coming back. What are they coming to do if our country is poor?" she asked. Her prayer to the country is for young people to stop abusing drugs and alcohol and instead turn to God.

From left to right Kibui Mutuanjeru, Nduhiu Wang'ombe, Mukami Kimathi, Gen Kihithuki and Nderitu Mukundi. The former freedom fighters had visited Mrs Kimathi at her Nairobi home in Kamarock Estate.

No more telling Mau Mau stories for free, vow Mau Mau War Veterans

By Muchemi Wachira

It is no longer an exciting prospect to talk about the struggle for Kenya's Independence for most of the ex-freedom fighters, which they once narrated with relish.

They are tired of repeating the same story for years but it ends up benefiting just a few people, who use it for self-congratulatory purposes after publishing newspaper articles or writing books.

On the other hand, the story of the freedom struggle has been hijacked by some con artists, who have, over the years, been using it for personal gain. They have successfully side-lined genuine freedom fighters who sacrificed their lives and time, waging war against the British Colonial authorities, from their hideouts in the forest.

Story of neglect

Unless a forum is created to address some of these issues specifically to help in distinguishing genuine freedom fighters from con artists, the history of Mau Mau and heroes of the liberation war may remain incomprehensible according to Macharia Mwangi alias Gen Kihithuki, Nduhiu Wang'ombe, Nderitu Mukundi and Kibui Mutuanjeru.

The four are among Mau Mau fighters who worked closely with Freedom war hero, Field Marshal Dedan Kimathi. And after being used by researchers, scholars and journalists to tell Kimathi's story and their exploits while in the forest, they have now vowed to remain mum.

"Let the story about Kimathi and the Mau Mau be brought to an end now until we get a better forum to narrate it," says Gen Kihithuki. He's believed to be one of the few surviving Mau Mau generals.

A visibly angry Mukundi, also known as Hang'arari, chips in - complaining that they have been used for long as a tool for giving information about the country's liberation war, by self-seeking individuals.

"We have been talking, talking and talking and those we give information publish books, they write newspaper articles and they're paid for their work! But what do we gain after telling our story?" the 91-year-old man whose right palm is almost dysfunctional as a result of a gunshot wound.

His right leg was also injured by a bullet and he walks with a pronounced limp. And in a polite tone, Wang'ombe alias Hungura explains that during national celebrations, organised to commemorate country's independence or to celebrate heroes day, radio stations usually invite them for talk shows.

"We give them our stories and our experiences while working with Dedan Kimathi who was our leader in the forest and after the talk show, no one bothers to even refund us fare back home," he recounts as his colleague Mutuanjeru chooses to remain silent over the issue.

Kimathi, the teacher and thespian

The scene is at the resident of Mukami Kimathi, in Nairobi's Komarock Estate, where the four aged men, who had close interaction with Dedan Kimathi had gathered to share their experiences in the forest with The Chronicles and what they know about Dedan.

He is the man who had discretely recruited them into the Kenya Land and Freedom Army (KLFA) that later came to be known as Mau Mau.

Both Mukundi and Wang'ombe hail from Karuna-ini Village where Kimathi also came from. While the latter is the nephew of the freedom hero, the former came into contact with the Field Marshal at local Karuna-ini Primary School.

Kimathi was a teacher at the school when Mukundi joined the institution for his early education. Besides being a teacher, the soon-to-be Mau Mau leader was also a thespian, whose fame

> "We give them our stories and our experiences while working with Dedan Kimathi who was our leader in the forest and after the talk show, no one bothers to even refund us fare back home,"

had spread across the neighbourhood, as people used to walk to Karunai-ini to watch productions Kimathi had produced, in the village.

He personally wrote plays and directed them – and during the performance he was always the main actor. His command of the English language and his commanding voice also distinguished him from other teachers.

Joining the Mau Mau War

Kimathi was to later employ Mukundi as a casual labourer at a European settler's farm in Ol Kalou area of Nyandarua (a district reserved for White Settlers), where he was the manager. It is from his admiration of Kimathi that he decided to join him in the Independence struggle.

After the Mau Mau War broke out and all the people associated with Kimathi were targeted by the Colonial authorities, Wang'ombe, he had no choice but to join the freedom struggle. He was only 18 years-old.

"Our homesteads were surrounded by home guards, forcing all the males to flee to avoid arrest," he says, adding that it was believed that all men, whatever their age, had taken the Mau Mau oath.

Mau Mau War veterans celebrate Dedan Kimathi 62nd Commemoration. The event was celebrated during a Gala Night at Uhuru Gardens in Nairobi early this year.

Mau Mau fighters assemble at Ruring'u Stadium in Nyeri to surrender their arms in December 1963 after the country attained independence.

Home guards were a paramilitary force comprising of Africans the British Colonial Government recruited to help them track down freedom fighters. Kihithuki became one of Kimathi's favourites, while in the bush.

Reason? Further from his curiosity, he was a swift and a prompt soldier who others had to rely on during incursions in the White settlers' farms. "I had worked at a white settler's farm in Mweiga and I was therefore familiar with such places.

Every time we were sent to raid settlers' farms to steal guns or livestock for food, Kimathi knew our battalion would not come empty handed," Thus the Field Marshal called him Kihithuki which literally means attacking by surprise.

He also recalls an incident where the Field Marshal had sent his three confidants, Inoi Kirugo, Gituku Kamaitha and Nderitu Emmanuel to Nairobi to get him his corduroy jacket. "The three were afraid to return to the forest with the jacket and Kimathi had to personally send me to collect it for him, which I did,"

Mutuanjeru known as Wa Nigro, during the Mau Mau War, had met Kimathi in 1943 in Nyahururu. They met at a white settler's farm near Lake Ol Bolosat, where his elder brother worked. His brother and Kimathi were close friends. Mutuanjeru was eager to join Mau Mau due for his admiration of Kimathi and in 1952 he crossed over into the forest through Chinga, Othaya – his home area -- to link up with Gen Mbaria Kaniu.

Photo session

Time is running out and the four men have to go back to Nyeri, when Mukundi learns that Wanjugu Kimathi, the Chief Executive Officer of Kimathi Foundation would not be joining them.

In her absence, he had vowed not to give The Chronicles team interview. He reluctantly opens up after Wanjugu, who was held up in a meeting, calls to assure them that it is okay to talk to us.

And the nonagenarian, who still looks strong, begins to tell his story though with caution.

All along, the host Mukami Kimathi - widow of slain Mau Mau hero - has silently been following events from her wheel chair at the far end of the sitting room.

She interjects- and on a light touch, narrates a story of colonial chief who was severely punished by Mau Mau adherents for betraying them after taking the oath. The chief, the aging widow continued, found himself in the custody of the Mau Mau.

"They told him they would not kill him but would inflict him with pain and leave a permanent scar he would live to remember. So, they cut-off the flesh of one of his buttocks and let him go." The story causes laughter and changes the mood in the house.

The stubborn Mukundi and his team who had earlier vowed not to pose for a photo session now come to an understanding. But no more discussions they insist - before calling it a day - promising to tell more dramatic incidents they encountered when fighting for freedom in the second issue of The Chronicles.

How war veterans were deliberately left out of land redistribution exercise

After losing their land in the course of agitating Kenya's freedom, Mau Mau veterans were caught in a vicious cycle, victims of shadowy political operatives, whom after Independence, were determined to reap where they did not sow.

By Gatu Mbaria

Why freedom fighters in Kenya were not given back land they were fighting to reclaim remains contentious.

And any attempt to respond to this question is bound to unearth layers of complications, British government's drive to have white settlers accommodated in the newly-independent country and the deliberate and consistent efforts by the Independence Government to keep ex-freedom fighters away from the main table, where the National Cake was being shared

According to an article, How the Mau Mau lost battle for land written in 2000, in the Daily Nation, Mau Mau freedom fighters anxiously awaited President Kenyatta's signal for them to overrun the white settlers' farms upon Kenya's independence in 1963.

"But instead, Kenyatta told the new nation that "hakuna cha bure" (nothing is for free), urging the Mau Mau and other Kenyans to "forgive (the white man) but don't forget." The article says that this reassured the white settlers who had sought to know whether 'their' farms were safe and that they could stay without fear.

It is apparent that the government of the late Mzee Jomo Kenyatta was quite keen to safeguard the land and other property forcefully taken from native Kenyans by the white settlers.

Kenyatta's policy appears to have been informed by the three major negotiations that took place at Lancaster House in January, 1960, February 1962 and September 1963.

Indeed, independence was achieved through what historian Prof Bethwell Ogot terms "a bargaining process between Africans and the two racial minorities, Europeans and Asians, with the British Colonial Secretary playing the role of umpire."

In his PhD Thesis, politician, Godfrey Gitahi (GG) Kariuki who is now deceased says that the land issues were part of the negotiations during the three conferences.

"European settler's main concern was guarantee of land titles and land values," he writes. To attain this, the settler group used a number of techniques during the negotiations, including penetrating and dividing African opinion, privatizing conflict and using administrative positions to control political initiatives.

The land problem mainly revolved around how to get back land forcibly seized by the White Settlers, who had alienated over 5 million acres by the start of the First World War.

Also under focus, was the question of what to do with the Gikuyu people, uprooted from their lands in Central Kenya and living as squatters in European farms in the Rift Valley, where they provided labour.

In a story written by journalist Kamau Ngotho, Michael Blundell, one of the land owners who became a politician in the Colonial Kenya, was instrumental in the negotiations and recommended that White Settlers who wished to remain in the country should not be forced to leave, but those who wanted to leave be allowed to dispose of their land on a willing-seller, willing-buyer arrangement.

Police assisted by home guards surround a village in hunt of Mau Mau fighters and their supporters at a village in Central Kenya/File

Ngotho explains that Blundell also came up with what was called the "One million-acre scheme" where the Independent Kenya government would be loaned money to buy land from the departing White farmers to resettle Africans in two categories of small-scale and large-scale land holders.

However, the land redistribution scheme was botched from the word go. The leadership of the new country was not interested in catering for the interests of ex-Mau Mau fighters.

Included too in this official neglect were millions of ordinary Kenyans. In this regard, Jaramogi Oginga Odinga, a leading nationalist leader and Kenya's first Vice President says in the book "Not Yet Uhuru" that at the end of the negotiation process, "leaders retreated from the people and hence the popular demands."

Odinga goes on to say that there emerged a small circle of leaders that was vulnerable to influence by forces that were against national interests. Together with leftist politician Bildad Kaggia and other leaders who shared his views, Odinga turned against Kenyatta and his administration especially because of their quest for redistribution of European-owned land, for the benefit of the poor people.

British Loan

The British Government had loaned the Kenyatta Government funds to carry out the land redistribution programme through the Settlement Fund Trustee.

According to a scholar, Purity Wanjiru Mwangi, the land settlement program was launched in 1961. One year later, the Department of Settlement was created to administer the program on behalf of Settlement Fund Trustee (SFT).

The latter was established under legal notice no. 352/63 of the Agriculture Act CAP 318, with the aim of resettling between 50,000 to 75,000 landless families.

By 1967, on a million acres in the former white highlands. The programme cost an equivalent to $77 million (Ksh7.7 billion) and was financed by Britain, West Germany, the International Bank for Reconstruction and Development and the British Commonwealth Development Corporation.

Interestingly, Kenyatta gave the job of dividing land and resettling Kenyans to a white man, the late Bruce MacKenzie, who then served as the Minister of Lands. The people settled on the white settlers' farms were given loans which they were to repay over time.

However, Kenyatta's policies angered many Mau Mau fighters. According to a story published by the New York Times shortly after independence, Kenyatta's land-acquisition policy attracted anger among the Mau Mau.

These were people who fought and died under a hail of bullets, while clutching a lump of soil, the ultimate symbol for the armed struggle. Many could not take this lying down.

"There have been secret oaths by a new terror society, the Kamau Maithori. It is an off-shoot, like the Mau Mau of Mr. Kenyatta's Kikuyu tribe," says the New York Times.

The Colonial Government started repressing the remaining Mau Mau fighters who refused to surrender when the State of Emergency came to an end in 1960.

According to a researcher, Anais Angelo, the Government's repression scheme was implemented between 1961 and 1965.

For instance, in Meru district (now Meru County), Mau Mau fighters gathered under the leadership of Field Marshalls Mwariama and Baimunge. Angelo quotes documents from the Kenyan National Archives, in particular, the correspondence of the Provincial Administration and security reports that said that politicians and officials regarded the remaining fighters in Meru as a potent political threat to the government of Jomo Kenyatta.

According to reports seen by this writer, Baimunge was killed in unexplained circumstances shortly after being promised 10,000 acres by Kenyatta, land which he did not receive. Besides ignoring their claims over land redistribution, the government started co-opting some of the Mau Mau leaders.

Angelo says Kenyatta carefully distanced the presidency from the government's choice of repressive politics. His government also organized what Angelo terms "symbolic propaganda campaign" with the aim of maintaining "the myth that Kenyatta had always been the Mau Mau leader the British arrested and jailed in 1953." In reality, Kenyatta had repeatedly denounced the movement.

Lost out "This is how we lost out" said a former freedom fighter who declined to be named. He expressed disappointment with the elite in Kenya saying they not only betrayed a noble cause but also created the individualism and selfishness that now cuts across people of different social strata.

"For us, we though the worst was over and long suffering of millions had come to an end. But we were soon to learn that our leaders had made a deal with the British at the Lancaster Constitution Conference.

They agreed to outlaw forceful takeover of the lands taken from us. I think the story of Kamau Maithori is the story of dashed hopes of most freedom fighters who took to the forest to free the country of the colonial yoke and force the return of the lands taken by the British mainly from the Gikuyu community," he concluded.

> Interestingly, Kenyatta gave the job of dividing land and resettling Kenyans to a white man, the late Bruce MacKenzie, who then served as the Minister of Lands. The people settled on the white settlers' farms were given loans which they were to repay over time.

How India's Nehru saved Kimathi's family from penury

By Muchemi Wachira

For the family of Field Marshal Dedan Kimathi Waciuri, accessing formal education, after the lifting of the State of Emergency in Kenya, was an uphill task.

Branded a dangerous terrorist following his arrest and eventual execution, no one wanted to be associated with Kimathi's family.

The widow of the slain freedom fighter, Eloise Mukami Kimathi had to struggle to get a permanent place to put up home for her children, which compelled her to seek help from well-wishers.

One of the well-wishers turned out to be former Indian Prime Minister, Jawaharial Nehru. A former freedom fighter and a member of the Indian Independence Movement, Nehru was a close friend to Kimathi.

"The two had met in Burma during the Second World War," Evelyn Wanjugu Kimathi, the last born daughter of Dedan Kimathi elucidates pointing out that the two freedom fighters found a common ground.

Kimathi is said to have led a mutiny after being conscripted into the King African Rifles to fight in Burma, when he questioned the move by British Authorities to place African soldiers at the front row during the War.

To him, the War had nothing to do with the people of Burma as it was primarily a quarrel between European Powers. Nehru was, at the time, actively involved in the Indian War of Independence.

Like in Kenya, Indians were fighting for self-rule from the British who had colonised them after occupying the Asian sub-continent, in 1856.

Through letters Kimathi used to write to the British Government and other humanitarian organisations, the world over, he made a name for himself. This is how freedom fighters like Nehru and Nelson Mandela, who was fighting the Apartheid Regime in South Africa came to know the Kenyan freedom fighter.

Eviction threats

So, when a row over ownership of three parcels of land Mukami had managed to secure through friends in Njabi-ini area of South Kinagop, in Nyandarua County flared up in the early days of Independence, Nehru decided to lend a helping hand to a family already in anguish.

Some tycoons in cahoots with officials at the Lands Ministry are said to have conspired to evict Kimathi's widow from her newly acquired properties.

The properties were being issued to new settlers through a loan advanced by the Settlement Fund Trust (SFT). The fund was a loan the British Government had advanced the newly independent government to carry-out a land redistribution programme.

Repaying the loan was a tall order for the widow and her young family. Founding Kenya's president, Mzee Jomo Kenyatta had to personally intervene to save the family from being evicted.

During this time, Mukami's first born son, Wachiuri Kimathi, his younger brother, Simon Maina and their two sisters – Rahab Wangechi and Elizabeth Nyankinyua were in primary school. With the burden of taking care of her four other children, their mother could not afford to support her entire family, especially paying school fees for her grown-up children.

President Kenyatta got her to be nominated to serve as a civic leader at defunct Nyandarua County Council but her earnings were still meagre.

Nehru, who died in 1964, had to

Former Indian Prime Minister, Jawaharlal Nehru

use his influence to secure a place at a children's home, owned by an Indian, in Parklands, Nairobi, for the three Kimathi children.

They would stay at the home and attend Arya Primary School. Julius Gikonyo Kiano, a minister in Kenyatta's government, according to the family, was also instrumental in securing a vacancy for the freedom hero's children to join the elite school.

After the eviction threat incident, not much was heard from Kimathi's. Even the whereabouts of the family had remained obscure until in the later years of Kenya's independence.

Mandela's visit

It is not until July 1990 when the family became the focus. Nelson Mandela had visited Kenya.

Mandela, who would later become South Africa's Independence president, had just come out of a 27-year imprisonment by the Apartheid Regime.

Apartheid was a policy, the South African Government used to isolate the majority or the Africans from the Whites who were minorities - making the former appear like lesser beings.

This was a form of racial discrimination and it was the similar policy used in other African counties including Kenya. Such exclusion prompted the indigenous people to raise against their colonisers either through violent protests or armed struggle.

In Kenya, Kimathi had led other freedom fighters in waging a guerrilla warfare against the British Colonial regime to recover land the colonisers had alienated after settling in the country.

Another objective of the war was to achieve independence as the foreign power had also imposed punitive laws after taking control of the country.

Mandela's disappointment

The war of independence in Kenya had won the hearts of other revolutionists across the African continent following the successive military campaigns the Mau Mau guerrillas used to launch against the British Colonial forces.

From their hideouts in the Aberdare and Mount Kenya forests, the insurgents would raid police stations and farms owned by European Settlers to steal guns and ammunition. Such bold and gallant operations are what emboldened revolutionaries like Mandela who were also trying to liberate their country from foreign domination.

Mau Mau had inspired the African National Congress' (ANC) military wing, Umkhhonto We Sizwe, Mandela had co-founded to fight the Apartheid Regime. Upon his release, Mandela accompanied by his then wife, Winnie, visited Kenya where, after they met President Moi, asked if they could visit Kimathi's grave as well as his widow and her children.

Mandela had made the request upon landing in Kenya in the company of his wife Winnie. The response he got from his host, Mr Moi is that Kimathi's Widow lived away from Nairobi.

> "We acknowledge our indebtedness to General Kimathi who led the armed struggle in this country against the British very excellently. And for that he paid with his dear life. Kimathi died but the spirit of liberation remains alive and that is why the people of Kenya are free today." (Daily Nation, July 14, 1990). Former South African President, Nelson Mandela

Former South African President, Nelson Mandela

Moi is said to have run short of words as he did not want to directly disclose to his visitor that Mau Mau was still an illegal movement in Kenya. So, if he wished to visit Kimathi's family, the Government would not be party to it.

Their wish was to first pay respect at the grave of the Mau Mau legend before visiting his widow. Mandela and his wife, Winnie did not hide their disappointment. After their meeting with Moi at State House, Nairobi, they addressed students at the University of Nairobi where the visitor, who was then the Deputy leader of the African National Congress (ANC) repeated the same message, expressing his wish to see Kimathi's widow.

And at a subsequent forum at Nairobi's Moi Sports Kasarani, the Mandela's expressed regrets that they were unable to see Kimathi family. In his speech Mandela said:

"We acknowledge out indebtedness to General Kimathi who led the armed struggle in this country against the British very excellently. And for that he paid with his dear life. Kimathi died but the spirit of liberation remains alive and that is why the people of Kenya are free today." (Daily Nation, July 14, 1990). Former South African President, Nelson Mandela

"We acknowledge out indebtedness to General Kimathi who led the armed struggle in this country against the British very excellently. And for that he paid with his dear life. Kimathi died but the spirit of liberation remains alive and that is why the people of Kenya are free today." (Nelson Mandela, Daily Nation, July 14, 1990).

Mukami meets Mandela

It was such a big embarrassment to the government and a disgrace to the country as Kimathi's remains were – as it is today – buried in an unmarked grave at Kamiti Maximum

Security Prison. There was no inclination by the Government of Moi or even his predecessor, Mzee Jomo Kenyatta to accord the Independence war hero any kind of recognition. To overcome the embarrassment, Moi directed two members of parliament – Muruthi Mureithi (Kieni) and his Dagoretti counterpart, Clement Gachanja to start tracing Kimathi's family.

Mureithi was not new to the Kimathi's as they came from the same village in Nyeri. His father, the late Mureithi Wa Wanjau was Kimathi's age mate.

He was also a colleague in a theatrical group Kimathi had organised, when he taught at Karuna-ini Primary School. Mureithi managed to find Mukami's younger brother, Mbuthia Wangome, who was working in Nairobi.

"I was working with the Kenya Commercial Bank as a driver at the bank's Industrial Area branch when Muruthi (Mureithi) came looking for me," recalls Wangome, adding that the MP gave him Ksh500 (approximately USD 5), as fare to go to his sister's residence in Njabi-ini, where she lived with her children, to ask her to travel to Nairobi to see the President. Mukami responded to the request by the President conveyed to her by her brother.

She travelled to Nairobi and went straight to State House where she met the Head of State. And he gave her the message from Mandela and his wife. According to Mrs Kimathi the explanation that Moi gave her for not allowing the South African leader of the liberation struggle to visit her is because the road leading to her home was bushy.

Government vehicles could therefore not accessed the place. Mandela's dream to meet with Kimathi's family only became possible during his next visit to Kenya when Mrs Kimathi was allowed to meet him at Presidential pavilion at the Jomo Kenyatta International Airport.

Dumped on roadside

Wangome recounts a similar incident when Mbiyu Koinange, a powerful minister in Kenyatta's cabinet, came looking for him. He too wanted to know where Kimathi's family lived, after he was asked the question in Parliament.

"It was in the early 1970's and I was a driver employed by the Kenya Bus Service. We had taken three of Kimathi's children to a centre in Nairobi owned by an Asian. The Asian was to help them access education as my sister (Mukami) was living in deplorable conditions,"

Unable to repay loans for her three parcels she had been thrown out of the farm by auctioneers before she sought help from President Kenyatta.

In those days, mentioning Kimathi's name, according to Wangome, was almost a crime. It thus took the intervention of one of Kenyatta's ministers, Julius Gikonyo Kiano, who secretly used his influence to help Kimathi children get registered as pupils at Arya Primary School.

It turned out to be a big surprise when Wangome was summoned by his general manager at the KBS headquarters, in Eastleigh, only to find Koinange in the office.

"I didn't expect such a guest to come looking for me," he relates and he further continues to recount: "I remember him telling me that an MP asked him to tell the house where the Kimathi family lived. He did not have answer and that's why he came looking for me. I told him that four of Kimathi's children were in a children's home and the rest were living with their mother upcountry."

That was the first and last communication, from the Government, on the position of Kimathi's family until Mandela's visit almost 20-years later.

A Mau Mau war veteran during Kimathi Day celebrations in Nyeri in February.

Mau Mau author, Karari Njama speaks during a function Dedan Kimathi Foundation had organised in Nairobi. Njama was Kimathi's personal secretary. His book "Mau Mau from Within" An Analysis of Kenya Peasant Revolt he co-authored with an American anthologists, Donald Barnett was published in 1968.

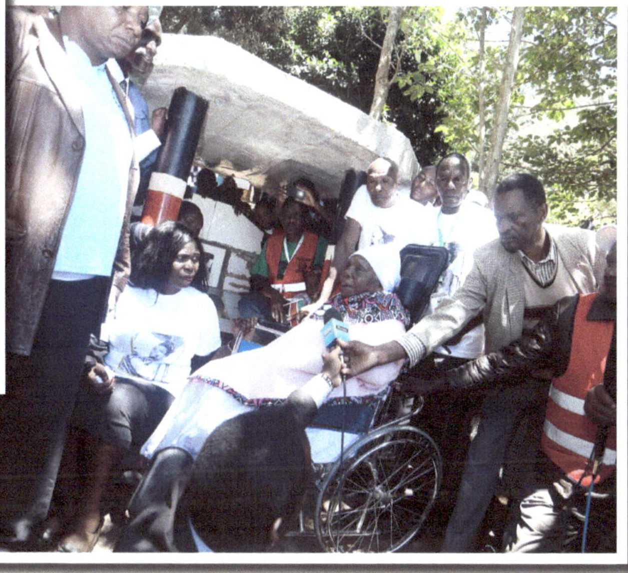

Dedan Kimathi widow, Mukami making her speech at Kahiga-ini Shrine in Tetu, Nyeri County during Kimathi Day last year. The day is celebrated annually.

A representative of Waiyaki Wa Hinga family speaks during Kimathi Day celebrations at Ruring'u Stadium in Nyeri.

A director of Dedan Kimathi Foundation, Mukami Githinji distributes foodstuffs to a group of women in Nyeri. As one of its social responsibilities, the foundation has been offering foodstuffs and other humanitarian assistance to needy families

Kiangai dancers from Kirinyaga County entertains guests during a function Dedan Kimathi Foundation had organised in Nairobi last year at Uhuru Gardens.

South African High Commissioner to Kenya, Koleka Anita Mqulwana (left) and Cabinet secretary Amina Mohammed (right) when they unveiled statues of former President Nelson Mandela and Field Marshal Dedan Kimathi at Dedan Kimathi University of Technology in Nyeri at the beginning of 2019.

A member of Dini Ya Msambwa in Bungoma County at Kahiga-ini Shrine in Nyeri during the commemoration of Dedan Kimathi 62nd anniversary

Kimathi's widow, Eloise Mukami (left) and Vuyisa Onabolu, second secretary, political at the South Africa High Commissioner's office in Kenya during Dedan Kimathi 62ndCommemoration Gala Night at Uhuru Gardens, Nairobi last year.

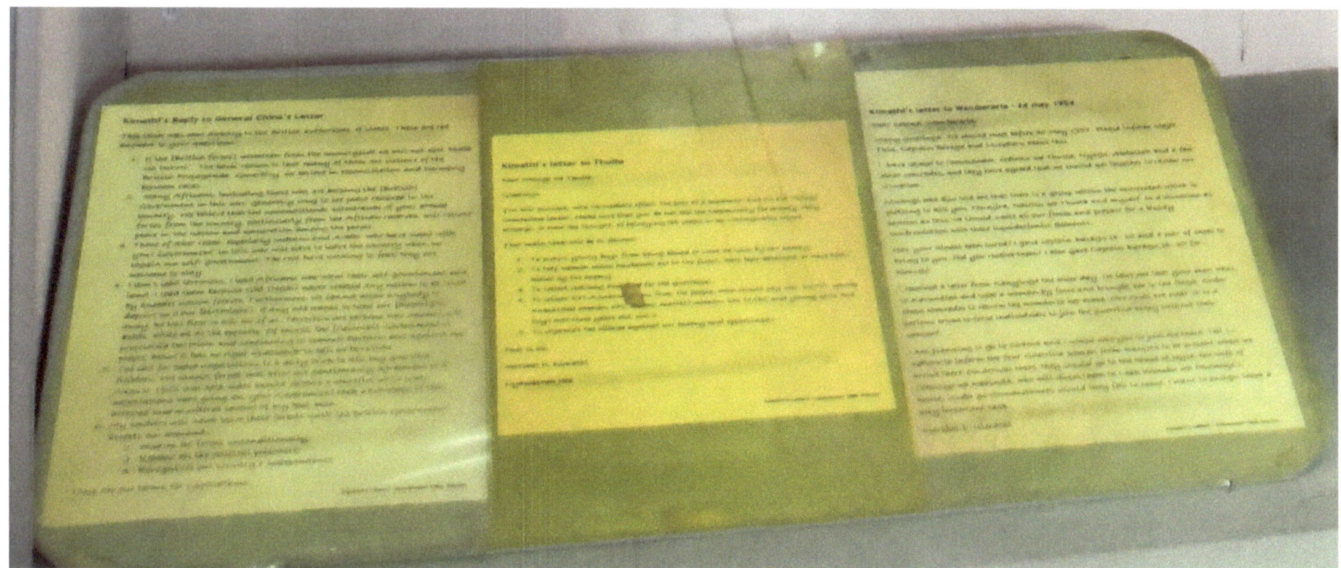

Dedan Kimathi's handwritten letters on display at the National Museums of Kenya.

WAR DISPATCHES: Field marshal would always organize his meetings at the edge of the Aberdare forest, bordering the villages

Letters from the bush: How liberation war was supported

In some of the letters, which have been preserved and are on display at the National Museums of Kenya, Kimathi discloses clandestine schemes the Mau Mau employed to mobilize support from villages

By Muchemi Wachira

Mau Mau activities were funded by members of the public who made personal contributions using an elaborate system that had been set up by leaders of the movement.

The system was only executed by the freedom fighters themselves, as the leader of the movement Dedan Kimathi revealed through his communication to his comrades in his hand-written letters. This was the commonly used means of communication in those days.

In some of the letters, which have been preserved and are on display at the National Museums of Kenya, Kimathi discloses clandestine schemes the Mau Mau employed to mobilize support from the communities in the villages.

The support was both moral and financial. The field marshal himself, the letters further reveal, would always organize his meetings at the edge of the Aberdare forest, bordering the villages. Villagers took the risk to attend such forums to discuss areas to be addressed to make the freedom war a success.

Kimathi also deployed his own men, in the villages where committee that coordinated Mau Mau activities were rife. Discipline was strictly observed in the forest, where the freedom fighters were bound by a code of ethics.

Here are selected excerpts from some of the letters Kimathi wrote to his fellow freedom fighters whom he had assigned special duties. In one of them, he talks about plans to eliminate him after his famous 1954 Mwathe meeting at Kabage Forest in Nyeri where he was crowned field Marshal of the Kenya Land and Freedom Army commonly known as the Mau Mau.

Letter to Wambararia A letter addressed to his younger brother Wambararia, who held a senior position in the Mau Mau movement, cautioned him that a plot was being hatched to eliminate them and other fighters loyal to him.

He wrote:

Dear Colonel Wambararia,
Many greetings. We should meet before 30 May 1954. Please inform Major Thia, Captain Baragu and Lt Gateru about this. I have talked to commander Ndiritu wa Thuita, Nyaga, Abdullah and a few other comrades, and they have agreed that we should get together to review our situation. Mwangi had also told me that there is a group within the movement which is plotting to kill you, Thunjira, Ndiritu wa Thuita and myself. In a situation as serious as this, we should unite all our forces and prepare for a bloody confrontation with these liquidationnists elements.

In the same letter, he continued to say:

I received a letter from Kanyinga the other day. He tells me that your men went to Karunaini and took a woman by force and brought her to the forest. Order these comrades to return the woman to her home. Our rules are clear: It's a serious crime to force individual to join the guerrilla army without their consent. I am planning to go to Chania and I would like you to join me there. Tell Lt Gateru to inform the four guerrilla women from Kanjora to be present when we arrive there. On arrival there, they should go to the house of Joyce the wife of Gikonyo wa Mahinda who will direct them to Leah Wambu wa Mutungi's house. Under no circumstances should they fail to come. I want to assign them a very important task.

There was also a letter he wrote to Maingi wa Thuita, a comrade deployed in the village:

You'll assume with immediate effect, the post of a headman and KLFA village committee leader. Make sure that you do not sell the community for money. Any attempt or even the thought of betraying the people is an unforgivable crime. Your main tasks will be as follows: To protect young boys from being killed or used as spies by our enemy. To help women whose husbands are in the forest, have been detained or have been killed by the enemy. To collect food and clothing by the guerillas. To collect KLFA subscriptions from the people. Men should pay Ksh62/50 (USD 0.56); young unmarried women Ksh32/50 (USD 0.29); married women Ksh11:50 (USD 0.10); and young boys and girls of over three years To organise the village against our enemy opportunists.

On accusations that he led a terrorist organization, Kimathi wrote:

"I don't lead terrorists, I lead Africans who want their self-government and land. I lead them because God (Ngai) never created any nation forever. Furthermore we cannot allow anybody to deprive us our (birthright). If anyone wants to take our (birthright) away, he has first to kill all of us. Terrorists are persons who commit evil deeds, while we do the opposite. Of course the (colonial) government is practicing terrorism and continues to commit barbaric acts against our people, hence it has no right whatsoever to call us terrorists."

The letter was in response to a memo written to him by Gen China (Wariuhiu Itote) who had been incarcerated following his capture in January 1954. He had told Kimathi that while chatting with an official of the British colonial government he had asked him why Kimathi led terrorists

Jomo Waiyaki, one of the great grand children of Waiyaki wa Hinga speaks during the interview.

Waiyaki wa Hinga: Heroic feats of a forgotten martyr

The rise to prominence of Waiyaki wa Hinga among the Gikuyu — and the genesis of the bad blood between him and the British that eventually cost him his life.

By Gatu Mbaria

The rise to prominence of Waiyaki wa Hinga among the Gikuyu — and the genesis of the bad blood between him and the British that eventually cost him his life.

They beat him up, broke his skull and tied him to a flag post, where he stayed overnight. In deep anguish and shivering from the biting cold of the night, the man persevered and refused to beg for mercy.

He was an extremely brave fighter, a just leader of men and a battle-hardened senior warrior. After waking up to the reality that white colonialists could not be trusted, the man had approached Fort Smith that day in a rage.

The guards on duty tried to stop him. But the extremely angry man drew his sword and fought them. They scampered for safety, paving the way for him to march on. Entirely consumed by anger, he was eager to unleash his wrath on the white man in charge of the fort.

As the story goes, the latter was then shaving his beard with the mirror facing the door. This enabled him to see the extremely tall and strong man in time as he lifted his sword to strike.

It seemed that luck was not on the side of Koiyaki ole Lemutaka (or Waiyaki wa Hinga) that day. This was on August 16, 1892, when Waiyaki stormed Fort Smith to kill Purkiss, who was in charge of the place.

The sword hit the roof of the fort, preventing him from slashing Purkiss to death. This gave the white man the opportunity to wrestle Waiyaki. As the two struggled, the ensuing commotion drew the attention of porters and friendly natives led by Kinyanjui wa Gathirimu, who rushed to assist Purkiss.

They then overpowered and wrestled Waiyaki to the ground. This gave Purkiss, a former sailor, an edge over the brave warrior. He landed a mighty blow on Waiyaki's head, causing him a severe injury on his skull.

Gathirimu, who was later appointed a colonial chief, is believed to have betrayed Waiyaki. "This is how Waiyaki met his fate," said Jomo Waiyaki, a fourth generation descendant of the legendary Waiyaki, who has done extensive research on the matter.

He says that Waiyaki had had enough of Purkiss and his retinue of armed porters, who organized one raid party after another against the Gikuyu people — stealing food and livestock, and molesting Gikuyu women.

Deportation to Mombasa

A day after one of the most important Kenyan heroes was arrested, the white people decided to deport him to Mombasa ostensibly to face charges in court. And so, with his arms tied to his back, he was escorted by a party of white soldiers and trusted Africans.

This was at a time when the Imperial British East African Company was in charge of Kenya on behalf of the British government.

Back then, many parts of the country were dominated by thick forests and had no proper roads. The railway was yet to reach Nairobi, and so the white colonialists and their retinue of porters would walk or ride on ox-drawn caravans from Mombasa to the interior.

This is how they made Waiyaki walk to Kibwezi, where they ended his life in a most bizarre manner on September 6, 1892.

As the party headed to Mombasa, word had already spread in many parts of Gikuyuland that the community's most respected muthamaki had been arrested by the white colonialists. There was tension in the entire Gikuyuland.

Warriors, who admired Waiyaki deeply, found this too big a provocation. It is said that the man was a caring, just and fearless leader of men who had earned the reverence of most members of the community after leading deadly assaults against Maasai warriors.

In one of the battles fought in Githunguri Gia Gichamu area (called Ngecha today in Limuru, Kiambu County), Waiyaki is said to have killed a lot of Maasai warriors.

In another battle staged in Ngong area of Kajiado County, the man killed Naleo, considered one of the fiercest and most troublesome of the Maasai warriors.

Naleo had organized one successful raid after another, killing many members of the Gikuyu community, stealing their cattle, and kidnapping some of their women and girls.

Up to the time Waiyaki took over the leadership of warriors, the Gikuyu had been unable to defeat Naleo and his band of warriors.

But Waiyaki, who inherited his bravery from his father, Kumale ole Lemutaka, led a vicious successful battle against Naleo that ended the latter's life.

His fame spread far and wide; the people resolved to make him their muthamaki and would give him the name "sultani". Some of the community members would travel all the way from Gakii (or Nyeri) to Uthiru in Kiambu, his place of residence, to pledge loyalty.

Waiyaki not hostile to British interests

Initially, he was not hostile to the British. According to the 1970 book, The Presbyterian Church in Kenya by R. Macpherson, his first encounter with the British was in 1887 when Count Teleki and his caravan arrived in Southern Kiambu.

The book says that Teleki was well received by Waiyaki. "In a solemn ceremony, Teleki and the members of his caravan took the oath of blood brotherhood with Waiyaki."

Later, Captain F.D. Lugard and George Wilson arrived in Kiawariua (present day Uthiru in Kiambu County) in October 1890. They, too, established good relations with Waiyaki, who also made a brotherhood pact with Lugard.

The two are said to have struck deep friendship and held each other highly. To cement it, they engaged in the blood-brotherhood ritual in Kihumo area where a PCEA church stands today. The ritual involved each cutting their own wrist and smearing a piece of roasted meat with their blood before each consumed the meat with the blood of the other.

"Following the ritual, they agreed that the Gikuyu would not only allow safe passage of Lugard's caravans but also that the white people would get foodstuffs from Gikuyu farms at a fee," says Jomo.

They also agreed that although Lugard would be allowed to construct a fort on Waiyaki's land in Dagoretti area in Nairobi, he had not bought the land.

This is how Dagoretti got its name (that is, from the Waiyaki's statement that "ndagūrīte gīthaka", or that "he did not buy the land").

Later, Lugard moved on to Uganda on November 1, 1890, leaving George Wilson to man the fort. But the roguish Wilson organized the looting of food and livestock, and molested women. "After the British broke the pact Waiyaki had made with Lugard, he attacked the fort," Jomo says.

The man staked his life to free his compatriots — and especially women — from routine raids by the British. But Wilson got wind of the impending attack and rapidly organized the burying of the supplies in the fort. When Waiyaki and his warriors arrived, they razed the fort to the ground.

Attacks and counterattacks

Macpherson says in his book that in the attacks and counterattacks that followed, 15 of Purkiss' porters mounted an operation to recover goats stolen from a local person friendly to the British from Githiga area, Kiambu County.

But when they tried to take back the animals by force, all but three were

Waiyaki granddaughter, Nelly Njeri Hinga.

killed by warriors. This led to a tit-for-tat attack during which 30 villages and all the crops therein were destroyed and 50 goats confiscated.

To Waiyaki, this was the last straw; he could take it no more. "It was after this attack that Waiyaki stormed the fort on his own, carrying his sword and rungu."He was to meet his fate that day".

On the day he was being escorted to Mombasa, Gikuyu warriors had woken up very early and travelled over long distances to confront the British. They caught up with Waiyaki's escort team at the place known today as Mukuru kwa Njenga. But just as they were about to attack, Waiyaki was to demonstrate his wisdom and selflessness when he pleaded with them to hold back and to return to their homes.

Reluctantly, they did so. Much later in the journey, the wound on Waiyaki's head developed serious complications and he would go no farther than Kibwezi, where the British are alleged to have buried him alive in an upside-down position.

"We are in the process of establishing where exactly he was buried so that we can give him a decent burial," Jomo told the Chronicles.

"Waiyaki became the first Gikuyu martyr… a song was later composed to remember his death," says MacPherson, who adds that the death of Waiyaki and other punitive actions by the Europeans "set in motion the disorganization of the Agikuyu democratic system of government."

Interestingly, as fate would have it, Purkiss was also to die in Kibwezi a year later. According to Macpherson, he "broke down in health" and died on his way to Mombasa. He was buried in the same ground as Waiyaki.

Family land, livestock grabbed

After Waiyaki was killed, his family suffered immensely and was to be in total disarray for about three years. His livestock and land were seized by the British.

This was at a time when the Church of Scotland was in the process of establishing a Christian footprint in Gikuyuland. Under D.C.R. Scott, the church wanted to be granted some 3,000 acres of land to set up not just the mission but also agricultural activities in order to sustain its operations.

Scott zeroed in on the land belonging to the Hinga family. Initially, this was denied as the law then stated that applicants could only be granted a maximum of 1,000 acres on freehold basis.

But Scott identified a loophole in the law by seeking the remaining 2,000 acres on leasehold basis. This was granted. But the church forgot one minor detail: It did not consult, and neither did it compensate the Hinga family.

> "Waiyaki became the first Gikuyu martyr… a song was later composed to remember his death," says MacPherson, who adds that the death of Waiyaki and other punitive actions by the Europeans "set in motion the disorganization of the Agikuyu democratic system of government."

This is the mistake descendants of Waiyaki have now zeroed in to stake a claim on the land that is now occupied by a host of Christian and public institutions. These include the Kikuyu Campus of the University of Nairobi, Presbyterian University Thogoto Teachers College, and PCEA Church of the Torch.

"We are claiming the land that was taken from our family by Scott," said Jomo, who serves as the Secretary of the Hinga Family Society.

Jomo adds that the family lodged the claim with the National Land Commission in 2016 seeking the return of the land or full compensation "Once the family placed the claim, NLC instituted a restriction barring the current occupants from selling or developing the said land until the claim is heard and determined."

However, the family is yet to make much headway following the dissolution of the NLC upon expiry of the former commissioners' term of office. Nevertheless, the matter calls to attention the serious historical injustices experienced by nearly all the families whose relatives stood up and fought against British colonisers to free the country of the colonial yoke.

It is also an indictment on the unwillingness of four successive post-independence governments to honour Waiyaki as a hero who pioneered the fight against the colonisers, not just in Kenya but elsewhere in East and Central Africa.

Nelson ole Reiyia Lemutaka from Sekenani area, Narok County is one of the descendants of Waiyaki wa Hinga.

Mau Mau monument at Uhuru Park. Known as Memorial to the Victims of Torture and Ill-treatment in the Colonial Era 1952 to 1960 it is located at Freedom Corner.